HEALING
&
RESTORATION

HEALING
Of the Body, the Bride and the Battalion

&

RESTORATION
Of A Royal Priesthood

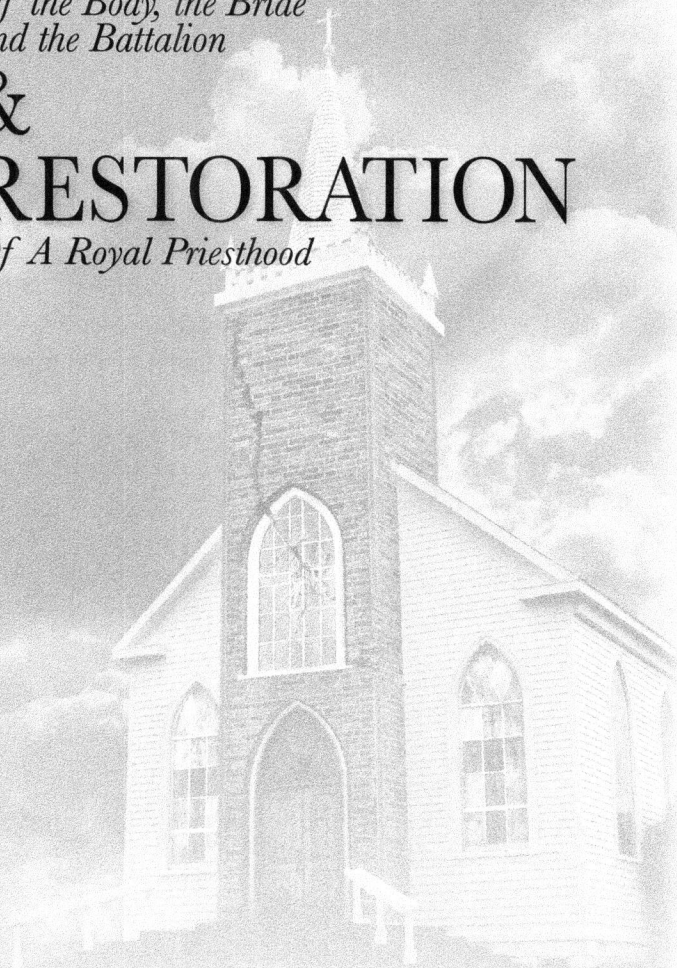

T.I. Fields

Table of Contents

Introduction

On April 29, 2008, I was asked to lead a prayer session. As I began to pray about the direction of the meeting, the Lord gave me specific instructions. He said, "I want you to declare this to be a year of healing and restoration!" Whether a year in God's time or our time, I don't know . . . yet it is time.

And the LORD answered me, and said, Write the vision, and make it plain upon tables, that he may run that readeth it.
Habakkuk 2:2

The Vision

God's Purpose

It was about the year 2005 when the Lord gave me a vision concerning the saints of God. One by one, I saw members of the church singing the song, "It is Well with My Soul."[1] As they sang the song, out of the other side of their mouth, they'd utter the truth about their lives. The song proceeded like this: "It . . . is . . . well"—but I hate my mother and my father—"with my soul!" Again, "It is well"—but I'm struggling with sexual perversion—"with my soul! It . . . is . . . well!—but my marriage is a mess—"with my soul!" On and on the vision continued. Then God flipped the title of the song and asked the church the question, "Is it well with your soul?"

The Lord began to reveal that many people had been living double lives and were struggling with hidden issues within their salvation. I could feel the pain and grief of the people. More importantly, I could feel that God was grieved, both by the people and for people. He said His people needed deliverance and that He was going to send it. It would be true deliverance, not just something that would "heal them slightly," as in Jeremiah 6:14 but one that would reach the core of the soul. It would be life-changing deliverance! God said that this deliverance would be twofold—bringing salvation for those who yield, and destruction for those who resist.

1

There was once a story told about the great Indian Ocean Tsunami of 2004, in which a minister caring for about twenty-five children was faced with that great wall of water. Rather than running from the wave, he decided to load all the children into a boat and steer to the top of it. Amazingly, he and the children rode that wave safely into the town. Yet the same wave that saved them, is the same wave that destroyed others. The Lord said we need to ride this wave of deliverance or be wiped out by it. It's either we will fall on the stone and be broken, or the same stone will crush us to powder (Matt. 21:44).

For the time has come that judgment must begin at the house of God: and if it first begin at us, what shall the end be of them that obey not the gospel of God?

1 Peter 4:17

God's Plan

The kingdom of God is established by spoken word. If we do not ask, we cannot receive. This is why Jesus told us to pray, "Thy kingdom come, Thy will be done in earth, as it is in heaven" (Matt. 6:10). Though He may have purposed it in the heavens, we have to speak it in the earth. Prayer is the key!

2 Chronicles 7:14 "If my people, which are called by my name, shall humble themselves, and pray, and seek my face, and turn from their wicked ways; then will I hear from heaven, and will forgive their sin, and will heal their land."

God said that in order for Him to send us deliverance, there must be a cry for it! The Lord said He was going to allow a great cry to arise in the earth, which would cause Him to respond with a great deliverance. He then gave me the Scripture in Jonah 2:2, which states, "I cried by reason of mine affliction." The Lord said He was going to allow the church to go through suffering, and that as the Chaldeans in the book of Habakkuk marched through the breadth of the land, so sin and suffering would march through the church (Hab. 1:6). I was aware but not prepared for, what I was about to see. I would get down in prayer and would hear the cries of the people and could feel their pain. In homes, in churches, and throughout the world, there seemed to be suffering and trouble all around. Like Habakkuk, I cried and asked the "Lord, How long?"

God's Process

I had hoped that The Lord would just look upon our pain, have pity, and make it all instantly better. Though few things in life, especially the things of God, just happen. No matter how brief or long lasting, there is always something that needs to be done first. It's what I call the "If-Then Process." Before we receive deliverance, we will pass through some phases:

1. Righteousness—God is first going to restore the righteousness of the church. In order for God to work, He must first restore the sanctity of the house.

2. Love—Once righteousness has been restored, the Spirit of God can flow from us and dwell amongst us. The greatest characteristic of God's Spirit is love, for God is love. First John 4:16 says, "God is love; and he that dwelleth in love dwelleth in God, and God in him."

3. Unity—Once the love of God is abiding with us, the peace of God will reunite us again. For the unity of

the Spirit is kept in the bond of peace (Eph. 4:3). Unity in the Spirit will allow God to flow freely amongst us.

4. Healing—Once unity has been restored and we are all on one accord, our connection in the Spirit will allow desperately needed healing to flow through the church; the body, the bride, and the battalion of Christ. For a bleeding body cannot function; a hurting bride cannot be intimate; and a wounded battalion cannot fight. It is time to arise and be healed!

    a. The Body- (Function): When the body is healed, it will function again. The gifts, ministries, and operations of the spiritual body will be restored.

    b. The Bride- (Intimacy): When the bride is healed, she can be intimate, conceive, and bring forth! Souls will be born through her deliverance.

    c. The Battalion-(Victory): When the spiritual army is healed, it will be reassembled and ready to fight the good fight of faith!

5   Restoration—Once we have been healed in all three of our major operative areas, we will function again as a royal priesthood and the kingdom will be restored.

PART I
Healing the Body, the Bride, and the Battalion

Project Life Line: The State of the Body

When the human body is injured or severely wounded, hemorrhaging (excessive bleeding) can occur. If it is not stopped, bodily functions and organs will begin to shut down—including the heart. Without an adequate amount of blood, the heart muscle, which keeps blood flowing through the body, will eventually stop pumping and the body will die. Leviticus 17:14 states that "the life of all flesh is in the blood," thus without blood, life cannot be sustained.

As it is in the natural, so it is in the spiritual. Just as the natural body needs blood flow for life, so the body of Christ needs the flow of the Spirit to live! The Bible says in John 6:63 that "it is the spirit that quickeneth" or makes alive. Unfortunately, the injuries we have suffered due to sin and satan have caused spiritual hemorrhaging. Yes! The body has been losing its "spiritual flow." Many have been running on such low levels of the Spirit they've become almost lifeless. In some cases the flow is so depleted we're in need of a spiritual blood transfusion! Without an adequate flow of God's Spirit, we as the body of Christ cannot survive . . . the body must be Spirit-filled and flowing!

5

There has been much damage, deterioration, and even dysfunction of vital organs, especially the "spiritual heart". Holiness is the heartbeat of the body of Christ. It's what gets that spiritual blood flowing! Without a strong heartbeat, adequate blood flow cannot reach the necessary organs and give life to the body.

This reduced flow of the Spirit due to a weak heartbeat of holiness, has even affected our "spiritual kidneys". Now in the natural, the job of the kidneys is to help purify the blood. They act as filters for everything passing through our bodies. Anything poisonous or toxic is checked by the kidneys. Unfortunately in some cases in the body of Christ, the kidneys have been shutting down and our blood toxicity has spiked! Our spiritual kidneys symbolize our convictions, standards, and sensitivities. These help to keep the body pure and free from the invasion of that which is toxic.

Due to the deteriorating condition of our kidneys, we've allowed everything and anything to get in—from negative music, media, and ideologies, to subtle spirits, sin and many contaminants of the world. This contamination has allowed us to become sickly, weak, and susceptible. Some have become so toxic there's a need for "spiritual dialysis." Kidney dialysis in the natural, is an attempt to cleanse and purify the blood, by use of machine, when the kidneys are not functioning. Some have lost their standards, guards, and sensitivities and simply need to revamp, recalibrate and repent! We need a revival of a true holiness movement!

We have got to get this heart muscle pumping again! Like the shock from an AED defibrillator, so the honest and unadulterated truth will jump-start that heartbeat. We must speak the truth in love, for the truth will help to bring life! (Eph. 4:15). Once the heartbeat of holiness has been regained, the spiritual blood will begin to flow and cause life, strength, and healing to return to the body. As the natural blood flow carries nutrients and oxygen through the body and transports waste from it, so the flow of the Spirit restores function, order, and health to the body of Christ.

Treatment and Recovery

When someone has been injured, one of the first steps to recovery is treating the wound. The only way to treat a wound is to expose it. Once it's been exposed, proper treatment can be administered. Covering an untreated wound can be life threatening. Bacteria can get in and cause severe infection, which can spread throughout the body, leading to extensive damage.

Again, as it is in the natural, so it is in the spiritual. The body of Christ has been wounded in many areas, often times due to sin. Our spiritual blood flow has been draining because of these wounds and they must be addressed. Exposing these wounds is the first step, but it's not enough. Ripping off a Band-Aid alone, doesn't heal a cut—it must be treated.

In March of 2007, I got down to pray. It was not about anything in particular, but simply to minister unto the Lord. After a few minutes of prayer and worship in the Spirit, something different began to happen, the tone of the prayer changed. My worship became ailing groans of pain. I suddenly grabbed the upper left side of my torso. I was spiritually bleeding, like I had been shot and the bullet was left lodged within me. I began to see flashes of past moments of my life and what I really looked like in the Spirit at those times. All that time, I was worshiping but wounded. I was working within the ministry but wounded. I was going on and living life yet bleeding from a spiritual wound. I was so stunned that this was my true condition all that time. I thought I was "all right." I thought I was strong. Sure, I had been through some rough battles on this Christian journey but I had no idea of the level of damage they had caused in the spirit realm.

As I continued to groan from the pain, the Lord reminded me of the medical explanation, that "it is more painful to remove a bullet than to leave it lodged in place." Then suddenly He pulled the bullet out! I cried out from the pain as blood gushed from my side in the spirit. Instantly God then plugged the bleeding wound with His index finger. The same finger He plugged it with, is the same finger He simultaneously stitched me with. It happened at once! The pain immediately stopped and I became calm and silent as the peace of God filled my soul and my room. As I layed there quietly weeping in the stillness of His presence, He then said to me "Now you can heal." He began to explain how I got the wound and what would have happened if He had allowed me to continue with it. He said I could not work effectively for Him like this. He had to treat my wound.

There was a message preached at our church in June of 2008 about the church being full of broken people. The preacher likened our lives unto broken "cisterns," that we keep trying to do a patch job and just move on. All I could think of was the body of Christ. We are hurt, injured, broken and bleeding but rather than deal with the issues, we keep limping on. Yet this is so detrimental to the future of our spiritual health. If we would just allow God to assess and address the damage, we could receive healing and truly move forward. If we continue to neglect the needful things, ultimately our progress will still be hindered. You can only run on a weak ankle for but so long.

We are the body of Christ and though we are made up of different members, we are all of the same body. We have suffered wounds in many different areas. Our degree of damage may differ, yet we all suffer, whether it's the leg that is hurt, the arm or the toe, the whole body is affected for it is the same body. So, while the head may not be injured, the neck might be. The hands may be wounded, but the feet may be fine. If your finger gets smashed, you do not look at it and say, "Oh, well! Nothing else is hurting." Rather, your hand wraps around that finger, and your mouth lets out a yell because of the pain response signaled by your brain. It's the entire body working together to be healed. Let us pray for healing of the entire body.

Function and Operation

When dealing with extensive wounds there can be internal damage—in particular, nerve damage. The natural body uses its nervous system to send electrical impulses to transmit information throughout the body. These nerves are connected at a specific point (space) called the "synapse" or "synaptic cleft." The Greek meaning of the word synapse is "clasp." It is because of the synapse that impulses are able to pass from one nerve cell to another. It is the connection between the nerves that allows for electrical impulses to pass throughout the body. If a message or signal is sent where nerves are damaged or disconnected, the flow of the impulse is blocked and the signal for operation or function is not carried out. For example if there is nerve damage in the foot, there will be lack of sensitivity or mobility in that foot.

9

As members of the body of Christ, we work like the neurons of the body. Ephesians 4:3 tells us to keep the unity of the Spirit in the bond of peace. That synaptic left or "clasp" in the natural, is representative of the bond of peace in the Spirit. This peace connects us as members of the spiritual body, just as the synapse connects neurons in the natural body. Our unity is important thus any break in our connection will hinder the flow of God's Spirit, and in turn, hinder our function as a body. We must be connected.

Nakedness: The Prerequisite for Intimacy

For Memorial Day, 2007, I prepared a message for a prayer meeting. The message was entitled, "Nakedness: The Prerequisite for Intimacy." In the message, the Lord said that He desired to have intimacy with His bride. However, intimacy requires that we open up and give him access to every area of our lives, allowing Him to see everything. Our level of exposure will determine our level of intimacy. Can you imagine someone attempting to be intimate while wearing layers of clothing? The more we reveal, the more access He can have.

As I meditated on the message, the Lord began to show me a person removing their garment before Him, and underneath was a bloody wound. I saw another person in a long white cloak and blood was seeping through their garment as they tried desperately to keep it covered. The Lord then gave me these Scriptures:

From the sole of the foot even unto the head there is no soundness in it; but wounds, and bruises, and putrifying sores: they have not been closed, neither bound up, neither mollified with ointment.

Isaiah 1:6

Come now, and let us reason together, saith the LORD: though your sins be as scarlet, they shall be as white as snow; though they be red like crimson, they shall be as wool.

Isaiah 1:18

The Lord said He wants to be intimate with His bride but not with her in this condition. He's a gentleman. She must be healed before engaging in intimacy. He said to let the people know that stripping is necessary, for underneath their garments are wounds that have not been tended to. He said He is the great physician and to tell them "The atmosphere is safe."

The next morning, as I stood before the congregation ready to deliver the message, I looked into the crowd and the Lord said, "They won't strip." I said within myself "What?" He spoke again, "They won't strip." I thought to myself, (impeccable timing). I then asked the Lord why? He responded, "Walk with me; I'm going to show you something." I knew within myself that this would be more of a journey than a walk. Since the message was now on "pause," I simply attempted to lead the congregation into spontaneous worship, while I scrambled to gather my thoughts (and my notes). I spent the following year taking notes as the Lord revealed why the bride wouldn't strip.

Comrades: The Battalion of Christ

From 1861-1865 America split and engaged in one of the worst wars in its history—the Civil War. Over one-half million men lost their lives. It was by far the bloodiest war America has ever fought. By 1865 the war had touched the lives of nearly every person living in the nation. What a catastrophe! North against South. American against fellow American. A nation divided. Can you

11

imagine, comrades at war, while their enemy could have come in to steal, kill, and destroy at any point? Oh, what a great destruction that would have been

So it is now within the church. The once united saints of Jesus Christ are engaged in a spiritual civil war. Brethren fighting against brethren. Arguments, bickering, competition, and contentions have built up walls of separation between us. Separation and division that have been produced by seeds of discord; discord sown by the enemy.

The great danger of discord is that it causes breeches in the Spirit, which both hinders the flow of God's Spirit and leave us open to attack. Yes! Our separation is leading to our destruction! We have been distracted from the real battle, with our real enemy. Rather than waging war against the enemy, we've brought the war right into our own camp. We've got comrades behaving like foes and brothers acting like strangers, while the true enemy has snuck in and launched his attack. As the rifts between us grow and the gaps widen, enemy access has been easier and more devastating. The statement still holds true: united we stand, but divided we fall.

Fallen Soldiers

We are soldiers in God's spiritual army, comrades fighting the same battle . . . the battle against sin and Satan. For some time now there has been a terrible onslaught of the enemy. Just as in Habakkuk 1:6, the Chaldeans have marched through the breadth of our land because of disobedience! The enemy has run rampant in our world, in our churches, in our homes and in our lives. Sin and suffering have affected us all one way or another. From the mighty to the feeble, from the leaders to the youth, no stone has been left unturned. If it's not personal suffering, it's the suffering of someone we know or love. There are soldiers MIA, numerous POWs and many have been wounded. There have been wounds incurred in personal battles, and wounds incurred fighting for others. Though we're wounded, we still continue to do battle yet how can a severely wounded battalion fight victoriously in a war? We are in desperate need of healing but none will cry out. Why?

Murderers!

Imagine soldiers wounded in a battle, bleeding from their injuries. They stand side by side and back to back on the same field, yet none will cry out for help. They choose rather, to suffer alone than to reveal their wounded state. Why would a soldier bear that kind of pain and suffering by themselves? The answer is fear. He is afraid because his fellow comrade has been found to be more than the foe. The one designated to have his back—the one assigned to stand beside him and cover him in battle. The one who should throw him over his shoulder and carry him back to safety in times of trouble, he has found may very we'll take his life. Worried that he'll be kicked, beaten stabbed, or shot, he quivers in the presence of his own brother. He's bleeding from the pain and it is slowly killing him. He is dying, but he's hiding, trying desperately to protect himself from the one ordained to keep him. He is even fearful of entering the safety camp because the place designated for rehabilitation and recovery has now become a war zone. Finding no place of rest, the wounded soldier chooses to suffer in silence. So it is within the church today. God said we have become murderers—in the house!

Whosoever hateth his brother is a murderer: and ye know that no murderer hath eternal life abiding in him.

1 John 3:15

Love worketh no ill to his neighbour.

Romans 13:10

We often do harm to one another as brethren. We at times have not been found to be trustworthy, upright, loving, or pure hearted with one another. When we ought to be destroying the enemy in each other's lives, we instead destroy our fellow man. When a soldier is wounded, instead of assistance he gets assaulted. When he is down, rather than being uplifted, he's trampled underfoot. Instead of being restored, he is destroyed or ignored. We no longer have bleeding hearts but rather we possess bloody hands . . . the blood of our brother!

In this kind of atmosphere, people are unwilling to expose their weaknesses. They are unwilling to admit their true state. No one is willing to show any signs of imperfection. No one wants to look like anything is wrong. We are so afraid of how we will be handled by our own brethren that even though we may be suffering, we dare not come forth!

This is not the atmosphere we were born in! It was once filled with liberty, love and safety! People were not afraid to bare all, to be broken publicly, or to show their weaknesses—because there was love, there was mercy. When someone was in trouble or had an issue, we quickly ran to assist out of a pure heart of love. God could often use a preacher to minister and call out needs and issues that were present within a service, now people fear their issue being revealed, so the man of God has difficulty ministering freely because of this fearful type of atmosphere. The Lord wants to minister publically that way again, not just to proclaim blessing and prophecy but to heal, deliver and deal with festering issues. An atmosphere of love, care and true concern for our fellow man must first be restored. We were once a people that rejoiced over recovery! Now we seem to delight in demise. It's no wonder we fear each other . . . but we're brethren?

Eliminating the Fear Factor

We've grown fearful of one another because of the way we treat each other. We have got to get rid of the fear amongst us. 1 John 4:18KJV " There is no fear in love; but perfect love casteth out fear because fear hath torment. He that feareth is not made perfect in love". The NLT says "Such love has no fear, because perfect love expels all fear. If we are afraid, it is for fear of punishment, and this shows that we have not fully experienced His perfect love." (1 John 4:18 NLT)

If people are afraid of us they have not yet been secured by our love. If we are fearful of one another, we may not be fully experiencing, nor expressing the love of God. The only way to attain that kind of love is through 1 John 2:5—"But whoso keepeth his word, in him verily is the love of God perfected." This means that if we are truly keeping the Word of God, the love of God will be perfected (matured to fullness) within us.

Brethren, it is important for us to make certain that we are striving to treat one another the way Christ would. We must aim to be pure in our motives and intentions toward each other. God has entrusted us with one another, how faithful have we been with each other?

15

Truly there are those, who even in the midst of love and safety are unfortunately so used to lack of love, abuse or condemnation that they dont trust anyone. There are also those with such deep seeded issues, it is very difficult for them to either give or receive love. Our job even then, is to continue to strive to love, to continue to show trust-worthiness, continue to be faithful and extend ourselves by the love of God. There are moments when we get the urge to do away with or disconnect from those that are difficult to deal with. Yet we have to remain, soft hearted and open handed, forgiving and forbearing. Only true love will cover a multitude of sins.

The love of God is what will help to set the right atmosphere because the wounded people around us, won't cry out until it is safe—and if it's not even safe for the saints, it certainly isn't safe for the sinner. God will not send dying people into a war zone. We've got to make it safe again!

Restoring the HIPAA Laws: Trust & Confidentiality

Our nation's health care system is guided by laws and privacy codes requiring confidentiality to help ensure safe and efficient patient care. These laws are known as HIPAA laws. The acronym stands for Health Insurance Portability and Accountability Act. Here is part of a statement from a medical privacy and confidentiality disclosure: (read carefully) "Once you give your written consent, we can use or disclose your protected health information for purposes of treatment . . ." (Garfunkel, Wild & Travis, P.C. 2002).

"Both the 1996 Congress and the two recent administrations agreed that a privacy law is needed to ensure that sensitive personal health information can be shared for core health activities, with safeguards in place to limit the inappropriate use and sharing of patient data" (CDT 2008).

"Individuals share a great deal of sensitive, personal information in the course of obtaining health care information . . . A substantial barrier to improving the quality of care and access to care is the lack of enforceable privacy rules" (Fox, et al. 2001). This information is then shared with others for many reasons. "Without adequate privacy protections, individuals take steps to shield themselves from harmful and intrusive uses of their health information, often at significant cost to their health" (NYS Department of Health 2007).

The church is considered a hospital for the hurting. Just as the staff of a medical health care facility has members, so we are the staff of a spiritual health care facility. We all have different responsibilities. Whether we are administrators, doctors, nurses, assistants, or maintenance workers, our one obligation is to the health care of the patient. We are held to a universal code of confidentiality with our patients and coworkers. We are required to maintain a safe and secure environment conducive to the healing of our patients. Just as in a medical hospital there are laws and rules in place for our patient's well-being, so it is in the spiritual hospital. Unfortunately, there has been a breaching of the code. In the natural it's referred to as a violation of the HIPAA laws. When health care professionals violate this code, it's usually at the expense of the patient's well-being.

In a hospital, the sole purpose of the exchange or disclosure of patient information is for treatment of the patient. A health care professional is not authorized to take confidential patient information to non-medical personnel or exchange information with personnel inappropriately. For example, a nurse—let's call her Betty—receives report on Patient A. With her eyes popped open she hurries into room 101 where Patient B her personal friend (and neighbor of Patient A) is staying. Nurse Betty shares all of Patient A's information with Patient B. They giggle over the news. Now we can see this is a clear violation of HIPAA. The information was not shared with necessary personnel, neither was it shared for the benefit of the patient involved.

Here's a second example: Dr. P has just seen a patient. After leaving the room, he calls up one of his colleagues to chitchat about the bizarre case he just had. He discusses the patient in a negative manner and discloses personal information. He discusses the patient with little care or sensitivity. This information was clearly not shared for the sake of the patient but for gossip.

As spiritual health care professionals, we must be careful not to spread confidential information that may be damaging to the persons involved. Any information shared must be toward edification, healing and recovery. We have been entrusted with the responsibility of patient confidentiality, which should be handled with much care. Violating the HIPAA laws can mean losing one's medical license along with other legal repercussions. The consequences for such actions are very serious. We must contemplate whether our actions will be beneficial or destructive to those in our care. Let us work toward restoration, not destruction. For if you stab your foot, you make it difficult for you to walk. If you cut off your ear, it will be difficult for you to hear. We are all members of the same body.

God has appointed us to assist Him in spiritual patient care. He has given us the tools to aide Him, but instead of using the scalpel to make an incision for surgery, we have used it to slice and dice one another to death. Many of us used to move in the gifts of the Spirit with clarity and precision but God has blocked us off because we have abused and misused our gifts. Our senses have gone dim, if not dormant . . . simply because we can't be trusted to do God's will only. We were once able to tell, able to see, we could sense each other. The Lord used to reveal things to us but we have used the gifts for intimidation, manipulation, condemnation and self-exaltation, rather than simply for edification, healing and restoration. This type of spiritual malpractice is against the law of God!

Due to this, God has raised up a people He can trust with His tools and His patients—spiritual health care professionals who He knows will do the medical work He requires. They will contribute to the wellness of the patients and abide by His codes.

Brethren, if a man be overtaken in a fault, ye which are spiritual, restore such an one in the spirit of meekness . . .

Galatians 6:1

In addition to patient care issues, we have personnel issues. We have a spiritual problem of contamination. We've got sick doctors, sick nurses, sick technicians. Isaiah 1:5 says . . ." the whole head is sick and the whole heart faint." In the natural, if a hospital, it's staff or one of its units is infectious, it would be shut down, quarantined, and decontaminated. So at times it is spiritually. In times of contamination and infection, we need to sit down in a season of sanctification, all for the sake of a healthy Spiritual environment. " For like a natural hospital, the atmosphere must be sterile and conducive for healing. God will not send the sickly and dying into our care until the right atmosphere is restored.

We must examine our spiritual condition first before we can truly deal with others. It is the spiritual truth that matters the most! It's not about what we display or portray, for "He that searcheth the hearts knoweth what is the mind of the Spirit" (Rom. 8:27). We must be mindful that God is looking at the heart. We ought to ask ourselves, if my heart and mind were on display, what would be seen? Would my thoughts toward my neighbor be right? Would my heart toward my brother be right? Let us strive to get it right. Let us aim not to destroy one another in deed, in word, or even in our thoughts. Let us remind ourselves of Psalm 19:14: "Let the words of my mouth, and the meditation of my heart, be acceptable in thy sight, O LORD, my strength, and my redeemer."

From Discord to One Accord

The birth of the church began in "one accord," not in discord. As we stated previously, discord has been sewn in our midst, by the enemy. There are breaches in many of our relationships because of unresolved (and even festering) issues. These breaches have split us apart, scattered us and made it easy for the enemy to attack us individually. God will not dwell in this kind of atmosphere, true unity must be restored!

When holiness according to God's word is restored, we will begin to express true love one toward another. Fear can be eliminated because love will leave no room for unforgiveness, malice, jealousy, hurt and anger, but will instead allow openness, honesty, humility, meekness, mercy, trust and forgiveness. This type of atmosphere promotes peace between us that binds us together in unity.

Once we are unified, God can send our healing and victory. We must understand that when we are disconnected, the flow of God's Spirit is blocked. It is through our connection that He flows. It's like an electrical cord, though plugged into a socket, if there are breaks in the cord, the flow of electricity will be interrupted. God wants to send us a corporate blessing, but it is going to take a corporate body . . . one heart, one mind, one voice.

There's a song by Hezekiah Walker called "I Need You to Survive."[2] (sing to yourself if you know it.) In it holds an essential message

PART II
Restoration of a Royal Priesthood

Set the House in Order!

From time to time, throughout scripture, God has raised up reformers who would take steps to restore true worship to the people of God, each movement marked by concern for holiness and the glory of the Lord.

Among these reformers were Solomon, Jehoash, and Josiah—kings of Judah—who repaired the damaged temple and restored priestly service and order. Zerubbabel who also led God's people in rebuilding, was aided by Ezra, who taught the people, and helped rebuild the city walls. What did all of these leaders have in common? Each leader sought the Lord ferverently before taking action. They moved to cleanse the land of idolatry and especially the house of God. It is this call to sanctification that leads us to focus on the actions of King Hezekiah.

The book of Second Chronicles, chapters 29 and 30, describes the reopening of the temple under the reign of Hezekiah. In it, we see the sanctification process and the reestablishment of the service of the sanctuary. We get to see the problems and hindrances to the progress of the work, and we also see the blessing and healing that came through obedience to the ordinances of old. Let us go through the text together; it reads as follows:

Second Chronicles 29:1-36

(1) Hezekiah began to reign when he was five and twenty years old, and he reigned nine and twenty years in Jerusalem. And his mother's name was Abijah, the daughter of Zechariah.

*(2) And he did that which was right in the sight of the LORD, **according to all that David his father had done.***

(3) He in the first year of his reign, in the first month, opened the doors of the house of the LORD, and repaired them.

*(4) And he brought in the **priests and the Levites**, and gathered them **together** into the **east street**,*

(5) And said unto them, Hear me, ye Levites, sanctify now yourselves, and sanctify the house of the LORD God of your fathers, and carry forth the filthiness out of the holy place.

(6) For our fathers have trespassed, and done that which was evil in the eyes of the LORD our God, and have forsaken him, and have turned away their faces from the habitation of the LORD, and turned their backs.

*(7) Also they have **shut up the doors of the porch, and put out the lamps,** and have **not burned incense nor offered burnt offerings in the holy place unto the God of Israel.***

(8) Wherefore the wrath of the LORD was upon Judah and Jerusalem, and he hath delivered them to trouble, to astonishment, and to hissing, as ye see with your eyes.

(9) For, lo, our fathers have fallen by the sword, and our sons and our daughters and our wives are in captivity for this.

(10) Now it is in mine heart to make a covenant with the LORD God of Israel, that his fierce wrath may turn away from us.

(11) **My sons, be not now negligent: for the LORD hath chosen you to stand before him, to serve him, and that ye should minister unto him, and burn incense.**

(12) Then **the Levites arose,** *Mahath the son of Amasai, and Joel the son of Azariah, of the sons of the Kohathites: and of the sons of Merari, Kish the son of Abdi, and Azariah the son of Jehalelel: and of the Gershonites; Joah the son of Zimmah, and Eden the son of Joah:*

(13) And of the sons of Elizaphan; Shimri, and Jeiel: and of the sons of Asaph; Zechariah, and Mattaniah:

(14) And of the sons of Heman; Jehiel, and Shimei: and of the sons of Jeduthun; Shemaiah, and Uzziel.

(15) **And they gathered their brethren, and sanctified themselves,** *and came, according to the commandment of the king, by the words of the LORD, to cleanse the house of the LORD.*

(16) And **the priests went into the inner part of the house of the LORD, to cleanse it,** *and brought out all the uncleanness that they found in the temple of the LORD* **into the court** *of the house of the LORD. And the Levites took it, to carry it* **out abroad into the brook Kidron.**

(17) Now they began on the first day of the first month to sanctify, and on the eighth day of the month came they to the porch of the LORD: so they sanctified the house of the LORD in eight days; and in the sixteenth day of the first month they made an end.

25

(18) Then they went in to Hezekiah the king, and said, **We have cleansed all the house of the LORD, and the altar of burnt offering, with all the vessels thereof, and the shewbread table, with all the vessels thereof.**

(19) Moreover all the vessels, which king Ahaz in his reign did cast away in his transgression, have we prepared and sanctified, and, behold, they are before the altar of the LORD.

(20) Then Hezekiah the king rose early, and gathered the rulers of the city, and went up to the house of the LORD.

(21) And they brought seven bullocks, and seven rams, and seven lambs, and seven he goats, for a sin offering for the kingdom, and for the sanctuary, and for Judah. And he commanded the priests the sons of Aaron to offer them on the altar of the LORD.

(22) So they killed the bullocks, and the priests received the blood, and sprinkled it on the altar: likewise, when they had killed the rams, they sprinkled the blood upon the altar: they killed also the lambs, and they sprinkled the blood upon the altar.

(23) And they brought forth the he goats for the sin offering before the king and the congregation; and they laid their hands upon them:

(24) And **the priests killed them, and they made reconciliation with their blood upon the altar, to make an atonement for all Israel:** *for the king commanded that the* **burnt offering** *and the sin offering should be made for all Israel.*

(25) And he set the Levites in the house of the LORD with cymbals, with psalteries, and with harps, according to the commandment

of David, and of Gad the king's seer, and Nathan the prophet: for so was the commandment of the LORD by his prophets.

(26) And the Levites stood with the instruments of David, and the priests with the trumpets.

(27) And Hezekiah commanded to offer the burnt offering upon the altar. **And when the burnt offering began, the song of the LORD began also with the trumpets, and with the instruments ordained by David king of Israel.**

(28) And all the **congregation worshipped,** *and the singers sang, and the trumpeters sounded: and all this continued until the burnt offering was finished.*

(29) And when they had made an end of offering, the king and all that were present with him bowed themselves, and **worshipped.**

(30) Moreover Hezekiah the king and the princes commanded the Levites to sing praise unto the LORD with the words of David, and of Asaph the seer. And they sang praises with gladness, and they bowed their heads and worshipped.

(31) Then Hezekiah answered and said, **Now ye have consecrated yourselves unto the LORD,** *come near and bring sacrifices and thank offerings into the house of the LORD. And the congregation brought in sacrifices and thank offerings;* **and as many as were of a free heart burnt offerings.**

(32) And the number of the burnt offerings, which the congregation brought, was threescore and ten bullocks, an hundred rams, and two hundred lambs: all these were for a burnt offering to the LORD.

(33) And the consecrated things were six hundred oxen and three thousand sheep.

(34) But the priests were too few, so that they could not flay all the burnt offerings: *wherefore their brethren the Levites did help them, till the work was ended, and until the other priests had* **sanctified themselves: for the Levites were more upright in heart to sanctify themselves than the priests.**

(35) And also the burnt offerings were in abundance, with the fat of the peace offerings, and the drink offerings for every burnt offering. **So the service of the house of the LORD was set in order.**

(36) And Hezekiah rejoiced, and all the people, that God had prepared the people: **for the thing was done suddenly.**

In the first year of his reign, Hezekiah repaired and cleansed the house of the Lord. This was in preparation for the service of the house, which was the work of atonement. The basic meaning of the word atonement is "reconciliation," thus they had the charge of the ministry of reconciliation. It was the job of the priests to perform the ministry of atonement. The Levites normally assisted them in this ministry, and generally served as judges, scribes, musicians, and keepers of the temple (Lockyer 1986, 644-645). This ministry was performed in three parts: atonement for the priests, for the nation (kingdom), and for the sanctuary. Atonement allowed Israel to celebrate the Passover, and with the Passover came their healing, restoration, and blessing.

Second Chronicles 30:1-27

(1) *And Hezekiah sent to all Israel and Judah, and wrote letters also to Ephraim and Manasseh, that they should come to the house of the LORD at Jerusalem, to keep the passover unto the LORD God of Israel.*

(2) *For the king had taken counsel, and his princes, and all the congregation in Jerusalem, to keep the passover in the second month.*

(3) *For they could not keep it at that time,* **because the priests had not sanctified themselves sufficiently, neither had the people gathered themselves together to Jerusalem.**

(4) *And the thing pleased the king and all the congregation.*

(5) *So they established a decree to make proclamation throughout all Israel, from Beersheba even to Dan, that they should come to keep the passover unto the LORD God of Israel at Jerusalem:* **for they had not done it of a long time in such sort as it was written.**

(6) *So the posts went with the letters from the king and his princes throughout all Israel and Judah, and according to the commandment of the king, saying, Ye children of Israel, turn again unto the LORD God of Abraham, Isaac, and Israel, and he will return to the remnant of you, that are escaped out of the hand of the kings of Assyria.*

(7) *And be not ye like your fathers, and like your brethren, which trespassed against the LORD God of their fathers, who therefore gave them up to desolation, as ye see.*

(8) Now be ye not stiffnecked, as your fathers were, but yield yourselves unto the LORD, and enter into his sanctuary, which he hath sanctified for ever: and serve the LORD your God, that the fierceness of his wrath may turn away from you.

(9) For if ye turn again unto the LORD, your brethren and your children shall find compassion before them that lead them captive, so that they shall come again into this land: for the LORD your God is gracious and merciful, and will not turn away his face from you, if ye return unto him.

(10) So the posts passed from city to city through the country of Ephraim and Manasseh even unto Zebulun: but they laughed them to scorn, and mocked them.

(11) Nevertheless divers of Asher and Manasseh and of Zebulun *humbled themselves,* and came to Jerusalem.

(12) Also in Judah the hand of God was to give them one heart to do the commandment of the king and of the princes, by the word of the LORD.

(13) And there assembled at Jerusalem much people to keep the feast of unleavened bread in the second month, *a very great congregation.*

(14) And they arose and took away the altars that were in Jerusalem, and all the altars for incense took they away, and *cast them into the brook Kidron.*

(15) Then they killed the passover on the fourteenth day of the second month: and the priests and the Levites were ashamed, and

sanctified themselves, **and brought in the burnt offerings into the house of the LORD.**

(16) **And they stood in their place after their manner, according to the law of Moses the man of God: the priests sprinkled the blood, which they received of the hand of the Levites.**

(17) **For there were many in the congregation that were not sanctified:** *therefore the Levites had the charge of the killing of the passovers for every one that was not clean, to sanctify them unto the LORD.*

(18) **For a multitude of the people, even many of Ephraim, and Manasseh, Issachar, and Zebulun, had not cleansed themselves, yet did they eat the passover otherwise than it was written. But Hezekiah prayed for them, saying, The good LORD pardon every one.**

(19) **That prepareth his heart to seek God, the LORD God of his fathers, though he be not cleansed according to the purification of the sanctuary.**

(20) **And the LORD hearkened to Hezekiah, and healed the people.**

(21) *And the children of Israel that were present at Jerusalem kept the feast of unleavened bread seven days with great gladness: and the Levites and the priests praised the LORD day by day, singing with loud instruments unto the LORD.*

(22) *And Hezekiah spake comfortably unto all the Levites that taught the good knowledge of the LORD: and they did eat throughout*

31

the feast seven days, offering peace offerings, and making confession to the LORD God of their fathers.

(23) And the whole assembly took counsel to keep other seven days: and they kept other seven days with gladness

(24) For Hezekiah king of Judah did give to the congregation a thousand bullocks and seven thousand sheep; and the princes gave to the congregation a thousand bullocks and ten thousand sheep: and a great number of priests sanctified themselves.

(25) And all the congregation of Judah, with the priests and the Levites, and all the congregation that came out of Israel, and the strangers that came out of the land of Israel, and that dwelt in Judah, rejoiced.

*(26) So **there was great joy in Jerusalem: for since the time of Solomon the son of David king of Israel there was not the like in Jerusalem.***

(27) Then the priests the Levites arose and blessed the people: and their voice was heard, and their prayer came up to his holy dwelling place, even unto heaven.

As we can see, the condition of priests eventually hindered the service of the house, thus causing the celebration of the Passover to be postponed (2 Chron. 29:16; 30:2-3). The significance of this is that the Passover was a time of great healing, blessing and deliverance for Israel. Similar to a new year, it symbolized new beginnings, but it only happened when the kingdom was sanctified and unified. In the previous chapter they had experienced sanctification, but not yet unification; their unity was just as important as their sanctity. It was normally celebrated in the first month of their calendar year, but had to be pushed back to the second month due to the condition of the priesthood and the scattered state of the kingdom and the people.

When they finally came together (though not totally), whosoever was willing and because of their leader standing in the gap in prayer and repentance and acknowledgement of their condition, they experienced great blessing, and healing. It was comparable to true revival in our day.

Although , this great celebration and blessing hinged upon the ministry of the house of God. The priesthood and the leadership had a direct effect on the kingdom and the people of the land. The ordinances have not changed; we must do the first things first. As Hezekiah ordered in 2 Chronicles 29:5, "Hear me, ye Levites, sanctify now yourselves, and sanctify the house of the LORD God of your fathers, and carry forth the filthiness out of the holy place."

Sanctify the Priests!
The Sin Offering and the Burnt Offering

Aaron and his sons were required to pass through a thorough consecration process before they were allowed to serve as priests (Exo. 29:1-46; Lev. 8:1-36). This process included ceremonial washings, investiture, and anointing with blood and oil. The priests were responsible for offering sacrifices, two of which were very important for sanctification and consecration: (1) a bullock as a sin offering, to put away their sin; and (2) a ram as a burnt offering, to indicate their full and complete surrender to God (Lev. 9:1-4).

During Hezekiah's call to the priesthood for restoration, he had commanded that both the sin offering and burnt offering be made for the atonement of all Israel, as in days of old (2 Chron. 29:24). The sin offering was a mandatory offering and was required annually for individual and congregational transgressions. The burnt offering, which was to be offered in the same place as the sin offering, was voluntary. This voluntary offering was the only sacrifice that was entirely consumed and was referred to as the "whole" burnt offering. It burned continually and it would last from morning to evening, or from one daily sacrifice to the next. It was also commanded that the fire on the altar should never go out. The emphasis, however, was not so much on the fire, but on the continual burning of an offering that was not to be removed. As the sacrifice lay on the altar burning, the aroma was to go up before the Lord as a sweet smelling savor. Once accepted, the fire of God would pour down and totally consume the sacrifice as a sign of its acceptance. This continual burnt offering represents an entire and perpetual consecration toward God.

As today's priests, the Lord requires the same offerings for sanctification; the ordinances have not changed. Romans 12:1 states, "I beseech you therefore, brethren, by the mercies of God, that ye present your bodies a living sacrifice, holy, acceptable unto God, which is your reasonable service." We are still required to present ourselves holy (sin offering) and acceptable (the burnt offering). Both are required for full sanctification yet so many of us have grown to a place and lifestyle of just daily repentance, leaving off the burning life of prayer. The sin offering alone is not enough; the burnt offering must follow. The Bible says that the sin offering and the burnt offering were to be slaughtered in the same place (Lev. 6:25).

Truly we ought to walk with a heart of repentance, striving daily to live a sin-free life. For "The heart is deceitful above all things, and desperately wicked: who can know it?" (Jer. 17:9). Our nature is so not like His. That is why David said, "Cleanse thou me from secret faults" (Psa. 19:12). Yes, some know how to abstain. No we won't touch the unclean thing, we've got that part down . . . the sin offering is on the altar! Yet what about the burnt offering? That voluntary offering that is supposed to burn continually before the Lord and not be removed from off the altar? The offering that was to remain there and burn until it sent up a sweet fragrance before The Lord. A sacrifice consumed by holy fire.

Do we still live that ever burning lifestyle? That fire filled life of prayer, that burns day and night? Are we still on fire for God? What does our life smell like to Him? Can He smell anything at all? Is our all still on the altar of sacrifice, or have we come down? What has moved us off the altar? What have we allowed to rob God of what is rightfully His? Is it sin, the cares of this world, busyness, etc.? These are the imperatives to ask and examine.

Unfortunately, like the priests in 2 Chronicles 30:3, many of us have fallen into a partial sanctification— yet both are needed for full consecration. We are well aware of what God requires and desires of us in our personal consecration. We know the necessity of the prayer life, the fasting and time in the Word of God it takes. Yet we have slacked up, put off, procrastinated, made excuses, and created substitutes, rather than offer up what is truly required. Many may not have to repent for living the way they shouldn't but instead for not living the way they should. We may have to repent for not living that burning lifestyle, for coming down from the altar of sacrifice. The thing is, the ordinances have not and will not change to accommodate our busy lifestyles or to assimilate with this world. Daily must we die, continually must we burn. It is our priestly, reasonable service. David said in Psalm 141:2, "Let my prayer be set forth before thee as incense; and the lifting up of my hands as the evening sacrifice." Let us burn in prayer and offer the lifted hands of surrendered lives, as an evening sacrifice.

This applies especially to those of us in leadership today. Just as the priests of chapter 29, we can find it easy to get to work in the house of God without operating in full consecration, living a busy life for The Lord, rather than a burning life for The Lord. This is so crucial because as leaders, we have the job of being sanctified—not just for ourselves, but also for the people. The priestly ministry is not just a position but also a duty by calling . . . a calling to stand in the gap for God's people. The priest must be chosen, sanctified according to ordinance, prepared to enter into the Holy of Holies—ready to stand before the Lord with clean hands and a pure heart and to bring back the glory and word of the Lord to the people. The weight of the ministry falls on the priesthood . . . and yes there is a weight! There is a yoke! The priesthood has a great responsibility. The Scripture says that to whom much is given, of him much is required (Luke 12:48). In order to truly perform our duties, our full consecration must be restored!

Then after we've washed and prayed for ourselves, do we earnestly and regularly stand in the gap in supplication and prayer for the people? A preacher by the name of Leonard Ravenhill once said, "To stand before men on behalf of God is one thing but to stand before God on behalf of men is something entirely different."[3]

Let the priests, the ministers of the LORD, weep between the porch and the altar, and let them say, Spare thy people, O LORD, and give not thine heritage to reproach, that the heathen should rule over them: wherefore should they say among the people, Where is their God? (Joel 2:17)

Nadab and Abihu: What is that Strange Fire?

And Aaron lifted up his hand toward the people, and blessed them, and came down from offering of the sin offering, and the burnt offering, and peace offerings. And Moses and Aaron went into the tabernacle of the congregation, and came out, and blessed the people: and the glory of the LORD appeared unto all the people. And there came a fire out from before the LORD, and consumed upon the altar the burnt offering and the fat: which when all the people saw, they shouted, and fell on their faces.

Leviticus 9:22-24

And Nadab and Abihu, the sons of Aaron, took either of them his censer, and put fire therein, and put incense thereon, and offered strange fire before the LORD, which he commanded them not. And there went out fire from the LORD, and devoured them, and they died before the LORD. Then Moses said unto Aaron, This is it that the LORD spake, saying, I will be sanctified in them that come nigh me, and before all the people I will be glorified. And Aaron held his peace.

Leviticus 10:1-3

In Leviticus 9, Aaron the high priest had performed his proper duties of sanctification, according to the commandment of the Lord. This sanctification was a must and was sanctioned by God's glory and presence. They offered the right sacrifice, God poured out fire and it caused the people to shout and fall on their faces in humility. In 2 Chronicles chapter 5, Solomon had prepared the temple according to ordinance and the glory of the Lord filled the house in such a way that the (sanctified) priests could not minister.

We too have had countless experiences of such glory and power of God. There have been many testimonies of people coming to altars and literally falling on their faces before the presence of the Lord. We have experiences of people being healed and delivered right before our eyes or being gloriously and powerfully filled with the Holy Ghost in mass numbers. We have been witnesses in times past of true out pourings of God's Spirit and have stood in His very presence.

Today, something different is happening. No more do we see as often, such moves of God. Like the elders in the book of Haggai, I'm sure our elders today would say "Who is left among you that saw this house in her first glory? and how do ye see it now? Is it not in your eyes in comparison of it as nothing?" (Haggai 2:3 KJV,) . In the book of Ezra 3:12 the scripture reads " But many of the priests and Levites and chiefs of the fathers, who were ancient men, that had seen the first house, when the foundation of this house was laid before their eyes, wept with a loud voice; and many shouted aloud for joy: " The experience was bittersweet. The temple was rebuilt but they had seen the former glory of Solomon's temple decades earlier, and it paled in comparison. I believe many of us in this generation can say the same . . . if we're honest.

Our encounters with God are not the same, the glory in the house of God is not the same, the singing, is not the same! The worship is not the same! The preaching, is not the same! The flow of the anointing, s not the same! The church is not the same! It is different now and unfortunately not always for the better. Yes we have more, we have increase, we have the new and improved, we have the greater and the excellent yet it's still not always . . . better.

For some the church has become a "network" based on talent, ability, influence and affluence. Let us be careful not to succumb to the world's system or pattern for the Kingdom of God. Lest we become like Esau, trading in our birthright for what is truly just morsel of bread. Remember it's the anointing that has always made the difference in our lives.

If we think back, we can remember things like all night prayer meetings, now we're ok if we get the church to pray for more than an hour. We can remember corporate fasting for days or more. Now if the church fasts for a day and together even, it's considered good. We used to see healings and deliverance more often when we prayed, now people walk in and out of our midst, at times untouched or unchanged. We used to cast out devils, now we don't even notice the demon possessed or we simply ignore or avoid the issue. People used to receive the baptism of the Holy Ghost with ease as God poured out now we sweat and toil for just one soul to pray through if at all. There are even those who have resorted to simply "pronouncing" people filled, sometimes for the sake of numbers and at times due to a lack of knowledge or spiritual discernment but this is about life and death, heaven or hell, it's too serious to play the numbers game. We have put away true prayerful intersession and altar work, because it's just that . . . work! We need people that are anointed and sensitive to the spiritual witness of the new birth; to entry into the body of Christ with the evidence of speaking in tongues. (See 1 Corinthians 12:13, Matthew 3:11, John 3:1-7, Acts 2:38, Acts 19: 2-6, Acts 8:14-17, Acts 10:44-48**) We need that kind of fire today! We need prayer warriors and intercessors again. We need altar workers that are kean enough to try the spirit and determine whether it be of God, of the flesh, or of the demonic. We need singers and musicians that minister before the presence of The Lord until His glory comes down. We need anointed preachers that will speak the pure word of God without fear or favor. We need the glory of the latter house to be greater than the former in these last days. That's what we need . . . but what do we have?

The Bible says that Nadab and Abihu took their censers (ceremonial vessels containing hot coals used for burning incense) and *put* fire therein, and *put* incense thereon and offered *strange fire*. This term *strange fire* or *unauthorized fire* refers to the fact that the coals for burning incense were not taken from the brazen altar of sacrifice, where they were supposed to be obtained. Aaron's sons decided to get it from another source, or in a manner that was not commanded by the Lord. When Aaron offered the sin and burnt offering for sanctification, fire *came out* from before the Lord, but Aaron's son's seemed to believe they could bypass the original ordinances (Lev. 9:24).

Like Nadab and Abihu, the priests of today have been presenting their own fire, working with their hands to produce that which God simply pours out. There's been an attempt to manipulate an atmosphere of glory by way of performance or stage show, using entertainment and ambiance to conjure up what only God can create.

To our next generation of leaders: we may desperately want revival, but it cannot be MANufactured. When we do this we end up with that which does not satisfy the soul or glorify God, we have to get our fire from the same altar of sacrifice, not strange or unauthorized fire. Our world goes for the quick and easy, but true revival takes time and work—real spiritual work. It's what I like to call "the background work." It will take the same fasting, the same prayer, the same study of the word, the same holiness, the same passion for souls, and true love for God and man. Once we have worked in the Spirit, we won't have to work so much in the natural because working in the Spirit makes the natural a lot easier! Entrance within the veil, by the power of incense and the atoning blood, brought Aaron into the very presence and glory of the Lord."[4]

So yes, this is a new generation, yes it's a new season and a new day, but the Lord said He would do a "new" thing not a "strange" thing. God still pours out fire from heaven! We don't need to fake it and we don't need to make it! We can experience that same glory, but it will take the same level of sacrifice.

My sons, be not now negligent: for the LORD hath chosen you to stand before him, to serve him, and that ye should minister unto him, and burn incense. (2 Chronicles 29: 11)

Hophni and Phineas
1 Samuel 2:12-17
(12) Now the sons of Eli were sons of Belial; they knew not the LORD.

(13) And the priests' custom with the people was, that, when any man offered sacrifice, the priest's servant came, while the flesh was in seething, with a fleshhook of three teeth in his hand;

(14) And he struck it into the pan, or kettle, or caldron, or pot; all that the fleshhook brought up the priest took for himself. So they did in Shiloh unto all the Israelites that came thither.

(15) Also before they burnt the fat, the priest's servant came, and said to the man that sacrificed, Give flesh to roast for the priest; for he will not have sodden flesh of thee, but raw.

(16) And if any man said unto him, Let them not fail to burn the fat presently, and then take as much as thy soul desireth; then he would answer him, Nay; but thou shalt give it me now: and if not, I will take it by force.

(17) Wherefore the sin of the young men was very great before the LORD: for men abhorred the offering of the LORD.

As I was musing over the sanctification process required for the priests, the Lord began to minister to me using the story of Hophni and Phineas. Often times we tend to focus on the fact that Hophni and Phineas were sons of Belial and that they lay with the women at the gate (1 Sam. 2:22). Indeed those were grievous offenses, but if we read carefully, the greater offense was the mishandling of the offering of The Lord. Due to this, the Bible states that the people abhorred the offering of the Lord. The word *abhor* means to detest; to hate, or to loathe. It originates from the Latin word *abhorrēre*, from *horrēre*, meaning "to shudder." The word *shudder* means to tremble or shake convulsively—especially as a result of fear or repugnance. The actions of Hophni and Phineas caused men to fear, despise, or loathe offering unto the Lord, so they kept back their offerings.

First Peter 2:9 tells us that we are the royal priesthood of today! The mishandling of the priesthood has caused many to abhor the offering of the Lord. People no longer want to come and offer up for fear of how they will be handled. Even as members of the church, we fear how we will be handled by one another, therefore no one will truly or freely offer up that which belongs to The Lord. If we are honest, we suffer from pretense, pride and fear. The problem with this is that there are many that really need to offer up the right sacrifice, whether the sin offering, the burnt offering or both but instead we hold back. Fear for their reputations, their name, how they'll be viewed, judged, treated etc. but holding back in our needed areas leaves us stuck in our condition. The fear of others has caused us to keep back from the one place we can receive help . . . the altar of sacrifice. The bible also says confession is good for the soul but if we are too afraid to open up, too afraid to pour out, too concerned about each other's opinions and less about what God is looking for, how then can we be helped? As members of the same body, priests of the same kingdom, we should be prepared, able, willing, loving and caring enough to allow one another to offer up freely and help with the sacrifice. We were called to each other, in love but fear reigns amongst us so many hold back their true offering. Where are the ready priests? Whose duty it is to receive and handle the offering according to ordinance.

The actions of the priesthood have a direct effect on the kingdom. We have the responsibility of dealing with people and their situations, yet have we followed the ordinance given to us? Have we been His representatives in the earth for His people? Or are we a generation like unto Hophni and Phineas?

Interestingly enough, the flesh hook they used to rob God of His offerings had three teeth or three prongs. The scripture in 1 John 2:15-16, came to mind which states: "Love not the world, neither the things that are in the world. If any man love the world, the love of the Father is not in him. For all that is in the world, the lust of the flesh, and the lust of the eyes, and the pride of Life, is not of the Father, but is of the world." Could the three teeth on that flesh hook be symbolic of the three worldly lusts? Could our motives and actions be driven by these fleshly natures? When people come with their offerings, do they have to deal with our three-pronged flesh hooks? Have we used our position, strength, authority, or influence to express or demand what God has not? The sacrifices of God are still a broken spirit and a contrite heart (Psa. 51:17). Have we let these natures of the flesh interfere with our priestly duty? Have we taken for ourselves the portion that belongs to God? The Lord says, "Get your flesh hook out of my pot!" Judgment is not our portion. Nor should we be a priesthood that operates to suit our own demands or to satiate personal appetites. It's not about what we want, but about what the Lord wants. It's not about what we think; it's about what God thinks. It's not about what we want to say but what He wants. Our duties must be performed according to the ordinance. Let us seek to have the heart and mind of the Lord toward His people and not our will but His be done. Let us take heed not repeat the same offenses as Hophni and Phineas. Let's remove our flesh hooks from God's offering pot! Eli reproved his sons for their offense in 1 Samuel 2:25, "If one man sin against another, the judge shall judge him: but if a man sin against the LORD, who shall intreat for him?"

Eli: The Father/The High Priest

Though Eli had done wrong, I considered the fact that God allowed Samuel to be raised up under his ministry. There were obviously some good things in Eli for the Lord to entrust him with Samuel. Eli was in tune with the voice of God. Eli's downfall, though, was that he wavered and allowed himself to be influenced by the flesh also. At times he was in the Spirit in his judgments, and at other times he was not. We can see this in his dealings with Hannah in 1 Samuel 1: 12: "And it came to pass as she continued praying before the Lord, that Eli *marked her mouth*." There Hannah was, praying with all her heart unto the Lord, and Eli looked at her (the carnal mind) and assumed that she was drunk. He initially judged her according to the natural. Later on, he dealt differently with her son, for the Bible says in 1 Samuel 3:8, "And the LORD called Samuel again the third time. And he arose and went to Eli, and said, Here am I; for thou didst call me. And Eli perceived that the LORD had called the child." The Bible says Eli "perceived" (the spiritual mind) that the Lord had called him. He was walking in the Spirit in this case with Samuel. God wants a priesthood that is going to do just as He says , with no wavering, no partiality, no personal preference, no flesh! It will take a concerted spiritual effort to walk in the Spirit. The bible tells us in Romans 8:5, 6 "For they that are after the flesh do mind the things of the flesh; but they that are after the Spirit the things of the Spirit. For to be carnally minded is death; but to be spiritually minded is life and peace. Though this isn't always easy and can even be very difficult at times, the priest must strive to do this at all times, in all cases, and with all people.

I share the following with much reservation and discretion:

One night I dreamt that I attended an event at a church service. A well known Pastor had invited a popular speaker to minister for his big revival service, there

was a large crowd. During the service, while preaching, the speaker stepped down from the pulpit through
the thick crowd at the altar and approached me as if
he was going to "declare the word of the Lord" to me.
However, he came rather close to me—right up to my
ear—and began to speak to me but very inappropriately.
While he was pretending to "speak a word" to me, he
glanced around to see if anyone was looking and then
began smooching at me. I was extremely uncomfortable,
but also very intimidated because he was supposed to
be a "man of God." I didn't know what to do . . . a feeling of paralyzing fear, helplessness and confusion came
over me. As I looked around to see if anyone could see
what he was doing, I noticed that the pastor was looking
right at us. He saw everything but said nothing. He knew
what was going on but chose to ignore it for the sake of
his "revival." There was too much at stake for him, so
he blew it off. I couldn't take it anymore and I ran to
the bathroom to pull myself together. My clothes had
been disheveled, my hair was a mess and I was crying.
I was so badly affected both inside and out. I could not
believe this could happen in the church. As I was pulling
myself together, and trying to straighten up, the pastor
came into the bathroom and into my stall and basically
tried to convince me to brush off what happened. I was
stunned! I then ran out and began searching frantically
for someone I could trust to confide in. I had a difficult
time finding anyone to talk to.

When I woke up from the dream, I was terribly dis-
turbed within my spirit. I began to analyze it. Deeply
troubled, I asked the Lord, "Is this occurring within in
the church?" He responded with the situation concerning Eli and his sons. It was clear that Eli did not agree

with his son's behavior but his relationship with them and what he was getting out of it interfered with his judgment. For the Bible says that though he "reproved" them (1Sam. 2:22-25), he did not "restrain" them (1 Sam. 3:13). It was Eli's job to both correct and chasten his sons but he did not. Due to this, God decided to reconstruct the priesthood.

And I will raise me up a faithful priest that shall do according to that which is in mine heart and in my mind: and I will build him a sure house; and he shall walk before mine anointed for ever.
1 Samuel 2:35

A Generation Unto the Lord

God said He was going to do away with the priesthood of Hophni and Phineas and raise up a priesthood like unto Samuel. Samuel was called in his youth. He learned to hear the voice of God at an early age. In various situations, Samuel was faced with choosing between his will and the will of God—but Samuel always yielded to what God wanted. Let's take a look at his decisions regarding different people in various instances from the Scripture:

Eli: And Samuel lay until the morning, and opened the doors of the house of the LORD. And Samuel feared to shew Eli the vision . . . And Samuel told him every whit, and hid nothing from him. And he said, it is the LORD: let him do what seemeth him good. (1 Samuel 3:15, 18)

When faced with fear and intimidation, (and though Eli threatened him) Samuel did what God wanted him to do. He could have allowed fear to influence him and shut his mouth, or held back part of the message, but he didn't. He spoke the whole truth.

47

Saul
1 Samuel 15:10-35 (Selected Verses)

(10) Then came the word of the LORD unto Samuel, saying,

(11) It repenteth me that I have set up Saul to be king: for he is turned back from following me, and hath not performed my commandments. And it grieved Samuel; and he cried unto the LORD all night.

(16) Then Samuel said unto Saul, Stay, and I will tell thee what the LORD hath said to me this night. And he said unto him, Say on.

(22) And Samuel said, Hath the LORD as great delight in burnt offerings and sacrifices, as in obeying the voice of the LORD? Behold, to obey is better than sacrifice, and to hearken than the fat of rams.

(23) For rebellion is as the sin of witchcraft, and stubbornness is as iniquity and idolatry. Because thou hast rejected the word of the LORD, he hath also rejected thee from being king.

(28) And Samuel said unto him, The LORD hath rent the kingdom of Israel from thee this day, and hath given it to a neighbour of thine, that is better than thou.

(35) And Samuel came no more to see Saul until the day of his death: nevertheless Samuel mourned for Saul: and the LORD repented that he had made Saul king over Israel.

In spite of Samuel's personal feelings and desire, he still did what God wanted. He did not allow his will to take precedence over God's will. We can see that Samuel had his own heart concerning the matter, for the Bible said he cried all night and mourned for Saul. He may have wanted Saul to remain king but it was not what God wanted. Samuel followed the will of the Lord.

David
1 Samuel 16:1-13 (Selected Verses)

(1)   And the LORD said unto Samuel, How long wilt thou mourn for Saul, seeing I have rejected him from reigning over Israel? fill thine horn with oil, and go, I will send thee to Jesse the Bethlehemite: for I have provided me a king among his sons.

(6)   And it came to pass, when they were come, that he looked on Eliab, and said, Surely the LORD'S anointed is before him.

(7)   But the LORD said unto Samuel, Look not on his countenance, or on the height of his stature; because I have refused him: for the LORD seeth not as man seeth; for man looketh on the outward appearance, but the LORD looketh on the heart.

(8)   Then Jesse called Abinadab, and made him pass before Samuel. And he said, Neither hath the LORD chosen this.

(9)   Then Jesse made Shammah to pass by. And he said, Neither hath the LORD chosen this.

(10) Again, Jesse made seven of his sons to pass before Samuel. And Samuel said unto Jesse, The LORD hath not chosen these.

(11) And Samuel said unto Jesse, Are here all thy children? And he said, There remaineth yet the youngest, and, behold, he keepeth the sheep. And Samuel said unto Jesse, Send and fetch him: for we will not sit down till he come hither.

*(12) And he sent, and brought him in. Now he was ruddy, and
withal of a beautiful countenance, and goodly to look to. And
the LORD said, Arise, anoint him: for this is he.*

*(13) Then Samuel took the horn of oil, and anointed him in the
midst of his brethren: and the Spirit of the LORD came upon
David from that day forward. So Samuel rose up, and went to
Ramah.*

In this situation, we see that Samuel also had his own
mind-set concerning the matter, yet he allowed God to
intercept his thoughts and thus he was able to proclaim,
"neither hath the Lord chosen this." Samuel did not allow
his perception to interfere with God's perspective. God
wants a priesthood after His own heart.

The priestly office was a very serious position, not to
be taken lightly. God was specific in the Law as to how
a priest was chosen and by whom the office should be
held. Not just anyone could serve, neither could service be
offered in just any old way. In 1 Kings 12, Jeroboam king
of Israel had breached the laws and ordinances concerning how the house of God was to be run and by whom,
and it caused Israel to fall into sin. Jeroboam's reasoning
for doing this was that he wanted to remain in control
and keep his position as king over the congregation. His
motives were self-centered rather than God-centered.
The Scripture reads:

*And he made an house of high places, and **made priests** of
**the lowest of the people, which were not of the sons of
Levi**. And Jeroboam ordained a feast in the eighth month, on the fifteenth day of the month, **like** unto the feast that is in Judah, and he
offered upon the altar. So did he in Bethel, sacrificing unto the calves*

*that **he had made**: and he placed in Bethel the priests of the high places which **he had made**. So he offered upon the altar **which he had made** in Bethel the fifteenth day of the eighth month, even in the month which **he had devised of his own heart**; and ordained a feast unto the children of Israel: and he offered upon the altar, and burnt incense.*

1 Kings 12:31-33

As we can see, Jeroboam did not follow God's leading in choosing priests nor did he follow the proper pattern for the house of God. He did what he wanted, when he wanted. He even came up with his own forms of worship and times of feasting for Israel, which were not according to ordinance. Today, ministers of the house are at times chosen because of talent, intellect, skills, connections, nepotism, money, social status, and many other reasons, rather than the main reason . . . being God-called, anointed, and appointed. Today, ministers are "hired" rather than called. John 10:13 says, The hireling fleeth, because he is an hireling, and careth not for the sheep. (John 10:13 KJV). One preacher declared emphatically, "ministry is not a profession, but a calling".

We must ask ourselves the question, how are our ministers chosen today? Did God call them or did they just look good to man, like the sons of Jesse. What of the days when people were prayerfully chosen, as in the book of Acts when the lot fell on Matthias and he was numbered with the eleven? (Acts 1:26). God still has chosen vessels whom He has prepared and ordained to serve in the priestly office. It is not by man's election but by God's selection.

As we can see, Jeroboam did not follow God's leading in choosing priests nor did he follow the proper pattern for the house of God. He did what he wanted, when he wanted. He even came up with his own forms of worship and times of feasting for Israel, which were not according to ordinance. Today, ministers of the house are at times chosen because of talent, intellect, skills, connections, nepotism, money, social status, and many other reasons, rather than the main reason . . . being God-called, anointed, and appointed. Today, ministers are "hired" rather than called. John 10:13 says, The hireling fleeth, because he is an hireling, and careth not for the sheep. (John 10:13 KJV). One preacher declared emphatically, "ministry is not a profession, but a calling".

We must ask ourselves the question, how are our ministers chosen today? Did God call them or did they just look good to man, like the sons of Jesse. What of the days when people were prayerfully chosen, as in the book of Acts when the lot fell on Matthias and he was numbered with the eleven? (Acts 1:26). God still has chosen vessels whom He has prepared and ordained to serve in the priestly office. It is not by man's election but by God's selection.

Sanctify the Altar!

In April of 2008, I dreamt I was standing in church before the altar. A sister ran up in front of the congregation speaking with tongues at the top of her voice. I was given the interpretation of what she was saying. She was reproving the church about its condition and beckoning us to arise. Then she turned to the altar with earnest pleading, and this was the interpretation: "Do you know what this altar would be like if it were sanctified?!" Suddenly, flashes appeared before me. People were coming up before the altar and they were being healed, filled, and delivered even before they got there. Miracles were happening! Then the voice of the Lord spoke and said, "There is not enough bloodshed on the altar."

When I woke up, I immediately went to the Scriptures where I had recently been researching information on the Levitical priesthood. In Exodus 29:37 it states, "Seven days thou shalt make an atonement for the altar, and sanctify it; and it shall be an altar most holy: whatsoever toucheth the altar shall be holy." This scripture was synonymous with the dream. Hebrews 9:22 says "And almost all things are by the law purged with blood . . ." The altar is sanctified by sacrificial blood. *"Romans 12:1 says "I beseech you therefore, brethren, by the mercies of God, that ye present your bodies a living sacrifice, holy, acceptable unto God, which is your reasonable service."* When we, the living sacrifices of today, repent and allow self to be slain upon the altar, we shed spiritual blood. That blood that is shed upon the altar is not only for personal atonement but it also sanctifies (purges) the altar. A sanctified altar sanctifies anything that touches it. When The Lord said there is not enough bloodshed upon the altar, He was revealing a lack of sacrificial offering upon the altar, in particular, the sin offering. Once the sin offering is offered, and the altar sanctified, the burnt offering is to be offered in the same place. When the aroma of the burnt offering is accepted, The Lord pours out consuming fire!

Now, we thank God for the ultimate sacrifice Jesus Christ our Lord, the lamb slain from the foundation of the world. We no longer need the blood of bulls and of goats as a sacrifice for our sin nor do we walk according to the law because we are now under grace by the covenant of the New Testament. We are the Ecclisia, the church, the spiritual Israel of today. 1 Peter 2:9 tells us that we are a royal priesthood and a holy nation and though we no longer live by the old natural requirements of the law, there are hidden spiritual ordinances and types and shadows of the Old Testament that still remain. Is the priesthood still living a sacrificial life? The temple of the Lord was a house of sacrifice! Yes it was bloody! Is the priesthood operating the same today?

In days of old, Atonement was made in three phases: atonement for the priests (Lev. 16:3-14); atonement for the sanctuary (Lev. 16:15) and atonement for the people (Lev.16:16-20, 23). Without atonement, Israel could not celebrate the Passover Feast and could not receive healing and deliverance. The Lord said in Exodus 12:13, "When I see the blood, I will pass over you."

God needs to see more bloodshed upon the altar. Yes our altars must be bloody! The altar is a place of slaughter , death to flesh and self where penitant, smitten, yielded hearts lay broken and totally surrendered before the Lord, but it's not happening much anymore. The true ministry of atonement, the sacrificial work of the house of God has ceased. God said the reason for this lack of sacrificial offering is found in Samuel 2:17 "For the people abhorred the offering of the Lord." They no longer want to come and offer up. Not because they don't desire to but because at the root, they are afraid to. The gravity of this is that the sin offering is mandatory—and if not made, the people remain in their sins.

In 1 Samuel 2:24, Eli reproved, "Nay, my sons; for it is no good report that I hear: ye make the LORD'S people to transgress."

Leprosy!

One day I was reading through my study material and as I turned the pages of one book, the titles on each page seemed to jump out at me with great force and a shout! The words read: "LEPROSY IN THE GARMENTS! LEPROSY IN THE HOUSES! "LEPROSY IN THE SANCTUARY!"

Leprosy (*tzaraath*, in Hebrew) was thought to be a highly contagious disease that could be spread even by touching someone's garment. It was imperative that the infected person show themselves to the priest in order for their condition to be properly assessed and addressed. Lepers were also required to acknowledge their condition publically by crying out "Unclean, unclean!" This was for the sake of those around them so as to prevent further contamination (Lev. 13:45).

The priest would declare a person unclean and the individual would have to remain quarantined until the leprosy was gone. After a certain period of time, the priest would reassess the leprous condition. If the leprosy was gone, the contaminated individual was declared clean and free to reenter society. If not, they were to remain quarantined until the priest saw that the disease was fully cleansed.

There are spiritual lepers in the house of God. Some are even aware of their leprous condition, but will not cry, "Unclean, unclean!" They are afraid. The problem is, the disease is spreading, and many others are being contaminated! Many are sick and spiritually contagious but none will cry out "unclean, unclean!" As in Luke 17:14, Jesus is saying, "Go shew yourselves unto the priest!"

The book of James 5:16 it states " Confess your faults one to another and pray one for another that ye may be healed." This verse is absolutely true and necessary, but we can't hold to this verse alone. Yes we must confess our faults one to another but there are times we must do as the preceding verse admonishes . . . go shew ourselves to the priest. There are some confessions that must be made to the man of God in our lives. Confession to your neighbor or confiding in a friend alone won't do. There are also those that hold only to "private, personal repentance" this is also valid and true and good practice. Though when it comes to some things, true repentance will breed confession. Confession may seem very difficult at times but if we can find the grace, strength and courage to despise the shame and get past the fear, it will unlock chains, release healing and ultimately bring restoration.

Due to fear, many won't show themselves to the priest. No I'm not talking about earthly doctrines and religious practices but it's the spiritual priest, the Pastor, the man of God who has been designated and ordained to help deal with the people of God. Let me sincerely declare, that no matter what, we can't bypass the order of God, we can't hide things, they can't be swept under a rug, for what is in darkness will come to light. The best thing to do is to repent, confess and be healed. If we really want to move forward in God, that's the way to truly get past it and get over it. That's the key to freedom.

What will help us to open up is having the assurance, of a priesthood we can trust. A priesthood that will do things purely according to ordinance. God needs a priesthood that is simply going to LET THEM COME, for they cannot remain in that condition any longer!

A priest should be forgiving, merciful, long suffering and filled with the love of God—not judgmental, able to deal with all the offerings that come. The priest should be impartial, not easily influenced or affected. A priest who has clean hands and a pure heart. A priest who has the mind and heart of God towards the people. Though this weighs heavily on leaders, once in the kingdom, we are all of this royal priesthood.

The priests of old had such an extraordinary job. They could somewhat tell what sin was committed by the type of sacrifice being offered. Yet no matter what was brought before them or who brought it, they had to keep a "straight face" so to speak. They had to have a washed, purified heart at all times. Nothing could get in the way of their responsibility of the service of the house, the kingdom, and the people of God.

There are times we try to do God's job of judgment, acceptance, and atonement, but we can't. There are moments we may be faced with people, pouring out issues that may be difficult to deal with, but no matter who they are or what they bring, our job is atonement. When handling them, we must be careful to follow the leading of God's Spirit and be mindful not to mishandle the offering of the Lord. We cannot be governed by our flesh. When we move from the carnal mind into the spiritual mind, we'll be amazed to see how God directs us. His ways are truly not our ways, neither His thoughts our thoughts (Isa. 55:8-9). In this we learn to not only walk with God, but to walk like God—to see what He sees, do what He does, and respond the way He would. It is not easy and can even be very difficult at times but when we respond according to the carnal mind, we are not doing our duty—and it affects the ministry, it affects the people, and it affects the kingdom. If we strive to live in the Spirit, we'll be less likely to walk in the flesh.

The job of the priest is exceptional. Like that of Moses and Christ, our high priest. We are the representatives of God in the earth for the people. First John 4:17 reads, "As He is, so are we in this world." Are we as He is?

But the priests were too few, so that they could not flay all the burnt offerings: wherefore their brethren the Levites did help them, till the work was ended, and until the other priests had sanctified themselves: for the Levites were more upright in heart to sanctify themselves than the priests

2 Chronicles 29:34

The Levites

According to 2 Chron. 29:34, the Levites had to step in and continue the work of atonement because there weren't enough sanctified priests to handle the job. It wasn't that there weren't enough priests, it's that there weren't enough sanctified priests to "flay" (to strip the skin off of/ prepare) the burnt offerings to burn before the Lord. I suspect this is not about numbers—but is about being capable of handling the burnt offerings. This is where the priests had the problem. The Levites were sanctified. They were truly prepared to handle all the offerings.

In these last days, God is going to send different kinds of people from all walks of life. Some even in our midst. They are coming with their problems and their issues. Will we be able to handle the offerings? They desire to be saved and they need God, but will we have the heart of God toward them or will our flesh get in the way?

We don't have a problem when people come in repentance, but when it comes to letting them move on and forward in God, we get stuck. When they are of free heart, surrendered and ready to be used, will we release them, or will they be blocked by our personal feelings and mind-sets? God accepts them. He is going to bring them in, clean them up, and have His way in them. Yes, she was a prostitute—but God wants to use her. Let her pass! Yes, they're of a different race or culture, but God has called them. Let them pass! Yes, he was a drunkard, but God has delivered him—let him pass! Yes, he was a thief, but God is going to turn him around, so let him pass! No matter what they were, when God delivers them, we must let them go! Revival is coming but we must be ready.

We must be able to allow people who have truly repented to move forward in God. We cannot hinder the kingdom! We are at all times to use wisdom in judgment but careful not to use our own wisdom. We must have the mind and heart of God toward the people. It takes a fully sanctified priest who is truly connected to God, walking in the Spirit to do that. That little trouble maker may become your best preacher. The one that was such a mess may be a diamond in the rough. That problematic one might be your greatest prayer warrior!

No matter who they are or what they have done, it is not our will but His will be done. When God gets ready, we have got to move or be moved!

The Levites were ready to do the work of atonement at God's command. The Levites are people that have the heart of God and will do His service and not be compromised by the flesh. They are only about the Fathers business. They aren't trying to build their own kingdom here, they labor only for His kingdom. Let our prayer be "Thy Kingdom come, Thy will be done."

The First and the Last
Matthew 20:1-16

*(1) For the kingdom of heaven is like unto a man that is an house-
holder, which went out early in the morning to hire labourers
into his vineyard.*

*(2) And when he had agreed with the labourers for a penny a day,
he sent them into his vineyard.*

*(3) And he went out about the third hour, and saw others standing
idle in the marketplace,*

*(4) And said unto them; Go ye also into the vineyard, and whatso-
ever is right I will give you. And they went their way.*

*(5) Again he went out about the sixth and ninth hour, and did
likewise.*

*(6) And about the eleventh hour he went out, and found others
standing idle, and saith unto them, Why stand ye here all the
day idle?*

*(7) They say unto him, Because no man hath hired us. He saith
unto them, Go ye also into the vineyard; and whatsoever is right,
that shall ye receive.*

*(8) So when even was come, the lord of the vineyard saith unto his
steward, Call the labourers, and give them their hire, beginning
from the last unto the first.*

*(9) And when they came that were hired about the eleventh hour,
they received every man a penny.*

60

(10) But when the first came, they supposed that they should have received more; and they likewise received every man a penny.

(11) And when they had received it, they murmured against the good-man of the house,

(12) Saying, These last have wrought but one hour, and thou hast made them equal unto us, which have borne the burden and heat of the day.

(13) But he answered one of them, and said, Friend, I do thee no wrong: didst not thou agree with me for a penny?

(14) Take that thine is, and go thy way: **I will give unto this last, even as unto thee.**

(15) Is it not lawful for me to do what I will with mine own? Is thine eye evil, because I am good?

(16) So the last shall be first, and the first last: for many be called, but few chosen.

God will raise up the feeble ones, the young ones, the new ones, and those who are considered "the least of these" to do His will. The most unlikely candidates, the " No Names". They are the David's of our day. They hold no special positions, and no royal blood runs through their veins, yet God has chosen and anointed them within our midst. God said, "I will use the foolish things to confound the wise" (1 Cor. 1:27, paraphrase).

The Elder Brother Syndrome
Luke 15:11-32

(11) And he said, A certain man had two sons:

(12) And the younger of them said to his father, Father, give me the portion of goods that falleth to me. And he divided unto them his living.

(13) And not many days after the younger son gathered all together, and took his journey into a far country, and there wasted his substance with riotous living.

(14) And when he had spent all, there arose a mighty famine in that land; and he began to be in want.

(15) And he went and joined himself to a citizen of that country; and he sent him into his fields to feed swine.

(16) And he would fain have filled his belly with the husks that the swine did eat: and no man gave unto him.

(17) And when he came to himself, he said, How many hired servants of my father's have bread enough and to spare, and I perish with hunger!

(18) I will arise and go to my father, and will say unto him, Father, I have sinned against heaven, and before thee,

(19) And am no more worthy to be called thy son: make me as one of thy hired servants.

(20) And he arose, and came to his father. But when he was yet a great way off, his father saw him, and had compassion, and ran, and fell on his neck, and kissed him.

(21) And the son said unto him, Father, I have sinned against heaven, and in thy sight, and am no more worthy to be called thy son.

(22) But the father said to his servants, Bring forth the best robe, and put it on him; and put a ring on his hand, and shoes on his feet:

(23) And bring hither the fatted calf, and kill it; and let us eat, and be merry:

(24) For this my son was dead, and is alive again; he was lost, and is found. And they began to be merry.

(25) Now his elder son `was in the field: and as he came and drew nigh to the house, he heard musick and dancing.

(26) And he called one of the servants, and asked what these things meant.

(27) And he said unto him, Thy brother is come; and thy father hath killed the fatted calf, because he hath received him safe and sound.

(28) And he was angry, and would not go in: therefore came his father out, and intreated him.

(29) And he answering said to his father, Lo, these many years do I serve thee, neither transgressed I at any time thy commandment: and yet thou never gavest me a kid, that I might make merry with my friends:

(30) But as soon as this thy son was come, which hath devoured thy living with harlots, thou hast killed for him the fatted calf.

(31) And he said unto him, Son, thou art ever with me, and all that I have is thine.

(32) It was meet that we should make merry, and be glad: for this thy brother was dead, and is alive again; and was lost, and is found.

We must be careful not to find ourselves in the condition of the elder brother. His anger over what he saw as an "injustice" or unfairness, produced feelings of bitterness toward his brother and resentment toward his father. This reached to such a degree that when it was time to join in the celebration for his brother, the Bible says "he would not go in." He was stuck and could not come to grips with his father's choice. We must be careful not to think of ourselves too highly, or as more qualified, greater, or better than others. For God will raise up the one whom we don't think "deserves it." The seemingly unqualified. We too, like the elder brother, can become stuck and unable to come to terms with God's choice. No matter what, it is not our will, but His will that must be done (Luke 22:42). It's all about His kingdom come, His will be done. In 1 Samuel 3:18, it was Eli who stood in judgment under the words of young Samuel, yet His response was: "It is the LORD: let him do what seemeth him good." He respected and accepted the will of God.

Celebrating the Passover Feast

God used the Levites to complete the work of atonement. Once the service of the house was set in order, God quickly prepared the people for the celebration of the Passover Feast. The feast was celebrated as a memorial for the great pardon and deliverance out of Egypt. It was to be kept on the fourteenth day of the first month (Tishri/ October) Due to the condition of the priesthood, the people weren't prepared nor unified and their feast had to be postponed. (2 Chron 30:2,3)

Hezekiah then had the task of reuniting the kingdom. Hezekiah made a plea for Israel to come together, for it was God's desire that the people be on one accord. Unfortunately, some of them ignored and rejected that plea—but there were those who humbled themselves and took heed.

So the posts passed from city to city through the country of Ephraim and Manasseh even unto Zebulun: but they laughed them to scorn, and mocked them. Nevertheless divers of Asher and Manasseh and of Zebulun humbled themselves, and came to Jerusalem. Also in Judah the hand of God was to give them one heart to do the commandment of the king and of the princes, by the word of the LORD.
2 Chronicles 30:10-12

For a multitude of the people, even many of Ephraim, and Manasseh, Issachar, and Zebulun, had not cleansed themselves, yet did they eat the passover otherwise than it was written. But Hezekiah prayed for them, saying, The good LORD pardon every one That prepareth his heart to seek God, the LORD God of his fathers, though he be not cleansed according to the purification of the sanctuary. And the LORD hearkened to Hezekiah, and healed the people.
2 Chronicles 30:18-20

This was a great task for Hezekiah, yet how simple was the solution to such a serious problem! What was it about Hezekiah's prayer that caused God to respond in such a manner? I believe it was Hezekiah's humble ability to work with whoever was willing, his honest acknowledgement of the true condition of the kingdom, and Hezekiah's contrite confession, a penitent plea for pardon, which was the key to God's answer and healing. Under his leadership, Israel went through proper sanctification and unification, and thus experienced healing and restoration. He restored the ordinances and God set His house in order and reestablished the kingdom.

Make it Plain

One night, about fifteen years ago, our church had a revival service outdoors. The Spirit of God was moving mightily. I was in a corner praying, and although we were having such an awesome move of the God, great grief flooded my spirit. It was as if I were in mourning over the body of Christ. I saw that the church was going to really go through. I saw trouble and chaos, but no way out. Overwhelmed, all I could do was weep and cry within myself, "The church! The church!" Suddenly, a sister came out of nowhere under the anointing of the Holy Ghost and grabbed a hold of me. Without me even telling her what I was feeling, she declared, "The church of the living God must move on!"

God is going to restore the kingdom, but it all starts with the priesthood! It is the priesthood that is responsible for the service of the house. If the priesthood is not in order, neither is the true ministry of the house of the Lord. The ministry of the church is not about positions, programs or crowds of people, it's a priesthood, with a true spiritual ministry unto The Lord. The condition of the priesthood has a domino effect on the kingdom that causes it to be either stagnant or progressive. The house must be set back in order, according to ordinance.

We need a priesthood that will come together in true sanctification and unification and will work to restore the true sacrificial ministry of the house of God, for the sake of the kingdom.

There will be priests in this last day that are and will arise. God always has a plan, and He always has a man. He is going to reconstruct the priesthood! (Matt. 16:18; Eph. 5:27). There is going to be (and has already been) a "changing of the guard," so to speak. For though He did away with Eli, He raised up a Samuel; and though there were priests that weren't sanctified, there was a set of Levites ready and able to do the service of the house. There will be a generation unto the Lord. God will have His way in us, in our churches and in our world . . . we will have revival! God will have a church to present before Himself without spot or wrinkle and against which the gates of hell will not prevail!

Church

We often cry out for souls in numbers and ask God for increase, but how He can He bless us with much if we are not faithful with few we have? If the members of the church cannot freely and safely pour out, how then can the broken hurting people of the world? If our own brethren aren't safe in our hands, how much more the stranger? God is preparing us for a great harvest. Is there someone with cleans hands and a pure heart who will reach out in love, to those in need? We are going to have to look through the eyes of God's love in order to see past their faces.

Heart to Heart

These words are not only for the members of church but for all people. There are homes, workplaces, friendships, relationships and individuals suffering but they won't cry out because they feel the need to protect themselves, their reputations, or their identities from others. There's very little trust amongst us but God did not intend for it to be this way. We ought to feel comfortable and safe with one another. A brother should be able to unveil himself to his brother, a sister to her sister, a husband to his wife, and a child to parents. Friends should be able to open up in times of need and say, "I'm in trouble. I'm broken. I'm wounded. I'm hurting. I'm scared. I'm weak. I messed up. I'm going through. I need your help, your support, I need you to survive. Instead we play strongman and princess perfect with one another.

There may be a member of your family in trouble right now! There may be a friend in desperate need right now! There may be a co-worker in danger right now! There maybe someone stressed and depressed around you. Yet they sit in silence, terrified to open up, not wanting anyone to know. They try desperately to protect their reputation or image, more concerned about how they will be handled or perceived, rather than if they'll be loved and cared for. This is certainly understandable, for if we have been gossipers, scorners, judgmental, mean spirited, backbiters, cold and uncaring, why would someone unveil their truth? Would you? It may be you, dying to open up, in need of help, strength, a listening ear, or a caring heart—but you find it so hard to reach out because you find it so hard to trust. So you sit with your issues, in your dilemma, with your drama, your weakness, your struggle, your pain or with that long festering problem in your life and you do it alone. You don't open up because you fear how damaging people can be and have been based on your experience. So you continue to wear the mask of pretense and you won't dare pull it down because this is how you survive . . . but God doesn't want you to just be a survivor, He wants you to be an overcomer and victorious!.. We need each other to do so. Yet there are so many things that come along to separate us from one another. Next to anger and un-forgiveness, competition and discord are two of our worst enemies. They keep us separated and always fighting each other. If we allow them to remain in our midst, we will never connect the way we should. Our unity holds such powerful blessings. We need to be able to connect with each other . . . and safely.

That pastor needs to be able to pour out! That husband needs to be free to bare it all! That wife needs to be able to say what's wrong! That young person needs to feel safe enough to tell all! There is a deep cry within! It is the cry that God responds to. There needs to be an atmosphere safe enough for the cry! The house of God is that place. This is the place where people can come and safely lay their burdens down, a place we can come and receive healing for our wounds, shelter from the storm. It's not a war zone but it's a place of rest. A place of love and care. This world offers so much pain and grief; there ought to be one place where one can find refuge. A safe haven. In days of old it was the only place where the penitent could find protection or receive amnesty from the accuser of their souls. It was referred to as the "sanctuary."

I'm reminded of a day I got a glimpse in the Spirit of tragedy coming to the earth, and many were affected—great and small, high and low. The only place they could run to was the church. They came flooding through our doors and the church was truly ready to receive them!

Even them will I bring to my holy mountain, and make them joyful in my house of prayer: their burnt offerings and their sacrifices shall be accepted upon mine altar; for mine house shall be called an house of prayer for all people.

Isaiah 56:7

Think on These Things

Isaiah 1:6, 18

Ezekiel 34

Habakkuk 3

Hosea 2

Jonah 2

John 13:34-35; 15:10, 12, 17

Romans 12:10; 13:8

1 Corinthians 13

Galatians 5:13-26

Ephesians 4:2

Philippians 4:8

1 Thessalonians 3:12; 4:9

Hebrews 10:24; 13:1

James 2:1-10, 15, 16; 3:14-18; 4:6-12, 15-21

1 Peter 1:22; 2:17; 3:8

2 Peter 1:7

1 John 2:3-6, 9-11; 3:3; 4

2 John 1:5

Endnotes

1. Horatio G. Spafford, "It is Well with My Soul," Music by Philip P. Bliss, 1873.

2. Hezekiah Walker and the Love Fellowship Choir, vocal performance of "I Need You to Survive," composed by David Frasier, on *Family Affair Vol. 2: Live at Radio City Music Hall*, recorded February 16, 2002, Verity, MR0000301462, compact disc.

3. Leonard Ravenhill. "Weeping Between the Porch and the Altar – Part 1," *Ravenhill*, 1994, http://www.ravenhill.org/weeping1.htm

4. Helen Hagan, "The Seven Feasts of Israel - Holy Convocations and Their Spiritual Meanings," Study 14, Heart of Israel, 2004. http://www.heartofisrael.net/mc/bible/7feasts/.

Bibliography

Center for Democracy and Technology. "Myths and Facts About HIPAA, Part 1." March 11, 2008. https://www.cdt.org/report/myths-and-facts-about-hipaa-part-1.

Clarke, Adam. "Commentary on Leviticus 8:1." *The Adam Clarke Commentary.* 1832. http://www.studylight.org/com/acc/view.cgi?bk=2&ch=8.

Connor, Kevin. *The Feasts of Israel.* Portland: City Bible Publishing, 1980.

Connor, Kevin, and Ken Malmin. *Interpreting the Scriptures: A Textbook on How to Interpret the Bible.* Portland: City Bible Publishing, 1983.

Dake, Finis J. *Annotated Reference Bible.* Lawrenceville: Dake Bible Sales, 1961-1991.

Fox, Susannah, Angela Choy, Janlori Goldman, Zoe Hudson, and Joy Pritts. "Exposed Online: The Federal Health Privacy Regulation and Internet User Impacts." Washington, DC: Pew Internet and American Life Project, 2001. http://www.pewinternet.org/Reports/2001/Exposed-Online-The-federal-health-privacy-regulation-and-Internet-user-impacts/Findings.aspx.

Freeman, James M. *The New Manners and Customs of the Bible*. Gainesville: Bridge-Logos Publishers, 1998. Rewritten and updated by Harold J. Chadwick. Gainesville: Bridge-Logos Publishers, 2001.

Garfunkel, Wild & Travis, P.C. "HIPAA Privacy Notice 01/07/03." *Medline*. 2002. Accessed October 1, 2013. http://www.medline.com/media/assets/pdf/HIPAA_Privacy_Notice.pdf.

Gill, John. "Commentary on Leviticus 8:1." *John Gill's Exposition of the Entire Bible*. 1748-1763, 1809. http://www.biblestudytools.com/commentaries/gills-exposition-of-the-bible/leviticus-8-14.html

Hagan, Helen. "The Seven Feasts of Israel - Holy Convocations and Their Spiritual Meanings." Study 14. *Heart of Israel*. December 3, 2004. http://www.heartofisrael.net/mc/bible/7feasts/.

Lockyer Sr., Herbert S., ed. "Levites" in *Nelson's Illustrated Bible Dictionary*. Nashville: Thomas Nelson Publishers, 1986.

National Committee on Vital Health Statistics. *Testimony of Janlori Goldman Before the NCVHS Subcommittee on Privacy and Confidentiality Regarding the HIPAA Privacy Regulation: Implementation, Compliance, and Impact on Health Care*. Washington, DC: HealthPrivacy.org., 2003. http://www.ncvhs.hhs.gov/031119p8.htm.

New York State Department of Health. "NY HISPC Final Assessment of Variation and Analysis of Solutions

Report." *Privacy and Security Solutions for Interoperable Health Information Exchange.* Albany: NYS Department of Health, 2007. http://library.ahima.org/xpedio/groups/public/documents/government/bok1_049439.pdf.

Ravenhill, Leonard. "Weeping Between the Porch and the Altar – Part 1." *Ravenhill.* 1994. http://www.ravenhill.org/weeping1.htm.

Walton, John H., Matthews, Victor H. and Mark W. Chavalas. *The IVP Bible Background Commentary: Old Testament.* Downers Grove, IL: InterVarsity Press, 2000.

Wikipedia. "Synapse." Last modified October 1, 2013. https://en.wikipedia.org/wiki/Synapse.

Sound Recordings
Walker, Hezekiah, and the Love Fellowship Choir. *Family Affair Vol. 2: Live at Radio City Music Hall.* Verity MR0000301462, 2002, compact disc. Recorded February 16, 2002.

Spafford, Horatio G. "It is Well with My Soul." Music by Philip P. Bliss, 1873. Public domain.

Author Biography

TISHANNA FIELDS is an anointed writer, singer and minister of God's Word. She currently serves wholeheartedly beside her husband, Pastor Damen Fields, as the first lady of Apostolic House of Prayer in Chapel Hill NC. They are the proud parents of four beautiful children, Jordan, Nathaniel, Aaron and Isrielle.

As an author, Sister Fields taps into the mind and heart of God as He powerfully uses her to express His truth. Among her greatest passions are fervent prayer and true revival in these last days. Bringing us impacting books such as *Healing & Restoration*, *The NoteBook* (2014) and *Breaking the Circle*; she stands as a latter day voice, crying in the wilderness of our world. Undoubtedly you will be provoked, stirred and blessed by this woman of God. She holds a BA in Theological Studies and is currently pursuing a Master's degree in Education.

www.ingramcontent.com/pod-product-compliance
Lightning Source LLC
Chambersburg PA
CBHW071626040426
42452CB00009B/1505